Expressions of a Life

Expressions of a Life

By

Danielle Rashea Brown

Library of Congress Control Number:		2021910508
ISBN:	Hardcover	978-1-6641-7429-0
	Softcover	978-1-6641-7453-5
	eBook	978-1-6641-7454-2

Print information available on the last page.

Rev. date: 06/08/2021

To order additional copies of this book, contact:
Xlibris
844-714-8691
www.Xlibris.com
Orders@Xlibris.com
830043

Contents

Acknowledgements

First, I would like to thank my dad, Herman L. Bass Jr., the man who supported me in all of my many endeavors. From the writing of these poems (which became my first book of poetry), to my dream of setting the modeling world on fire (remember that haircut, dad?!) Well, you supported most of my endeavors, lol, and my many business ventures. Dad, you were my compass when I needed direction. I didn't always know the path that I was to take, but you prepared me for the journey. I thank you for being the father that I needed and for all the valuable life lessons. And you gave them to us straight, no chaser!! Love you dad! To my sister Annette L. Owens, the troubleshooter, for you always had the answer to the who, the what, the where and the how. Thank you for encouraging me to share my work with the world, that I might be an inspiration to others. Good lookin' out, sis! Herman L. Bass III, my brother, and the only person I know who is "Excellent!" all the time! I admire your tenacity, your spirit and your business savvy…it is ELECTRIFYING!!! Keep hope alive lil' bro! To my aunt Marian, you have been just everything to me: my mother, my girlfriend, my sister, an older version of myself, my grieving partner for we have lost many, and a living legacy that connects me to those I have never met, but are so much a part of who I am. I cherish you. Lisa, surprise!! From as far back as I can remember, you have always supported this gift of writing and kept encouraging me to get my book published. I really wish I had listened to you and done this sooner. Thank you for being you all the time. I love you just the way you are! Dee, we've shared some places and spaces together. You may be far in distance but I keep you close in my heart. Thank you for all of the insightful conversations. Love you lil' cuz! To my grown up baby boys Earl and Charles (Buddha), you will always be my baby boys. I love you both so much and I am proud of you both as your lives continue to evolve into the young men GOD has destined you to be. I can't wait to see what He will do in your young lives next. Just keep Him first. To Anika, the precious little girl GOD blessed me with when she was only 4 years old. Anika, you were the little girl I always wanted, yet never had. I adored you then and still do to this day. Thank you for the joy you have brought me over the years and for being the daughter I always wanted. I love you. Jasmine, how could I leave you out? From the first day I met your bubbly, effervescent personality, you have been like a breath of fresh air in the springtime. Always delightful. You never fail to put a smile on my face because there is always one on yours. I love you like a daughter. To the memory of my cousin Sally, I wish we could be the way we were when we were young, then I would have had more time with you. I really miss you. Last but not least (I didn't forget you honey), to my husband Charles, now you see what I have been doing behind that closed door. You always see in me qualities I refuse to see in myself and you have been my greatest supporter. I love you for the man and husband that you are. You are truly my knight in armor.

Ultimately, I give thanks to GOD, the Creator of all things, for without Him this book would not exist. To GOD Be the Glory.

Dedication

I dedicate this book to the memory of my mom, Clara Jean Bass. Mom, it seems like a lifetime ago that we were together as mother and daughter. It was a lifetime, yours. Most of the poems in this book were written during a time when I wanted to be me; good, bad or indifferent. In the midst of our relationship, you were always there for me to confide in and to share my life with as it were, but I chose to put all those thoughts, feelings, joys, pains, questions, disappointments, memories, triumphs and tears into words that make up the poems in this book.

I understand that there were times you were not capable of appreciating the young woman I needed to be, and there were times I wouldn't allow you to be the mother you needed to be. We both needed each other, but it was those dark places within the both of us that prevented us from appreciating each other's light. I thank GOD for the gift of writing, Mom, because it allowed me to express myself and that's what I needed most. My greatest regret is that I did not share more of myself with you, but my greatest joy is knowing that GOD knew what we needed and made provisions for us both.

I never thought I'd ever be without you.

I am not a river
closer to a stream
I believe in fantasies
nurturing my dreams
When I entertain words
they give me a song
but in art of poetry
my words belong.

Universal

Where does it say in the stars
tomorrow will forever come
why for tell the future
when stars fade one by one

Darkness lights another heavenly body
emphasizing the need to create
an illustrious change of universe
distinguish a character ever so great

Beauty, in the horizon's unity
not a oneness but all complete
together a harmony of Divine serenity
where wild and peaceful only come to meet

Across the galaxy there's a hold
of another born into untamable thirsts
adventurous reverie becomes a part
of a celestial body and one from earth

Sun signs influence our personal world
transitional planets give them cause to be
seek a treasure there lies a fortune
within a Libran, balanced uniquely

The Virgin is the heart of purity
with her share of moody demands
the twins are as individual as
a woman independent of a man

The crab cannot be swayed from its cove
his shell is a mighty hard one
the Aquarian is in the age of herself
with years of knowledge and wisdom

Tonight, I'll catch a falling star
a message from above
be intrigued by your myriad discoveries
of the universe and the world thereof.

Aquarian Sister

I see a heavenly star, silently
her guardian angel appears
To bless the child for now she rests
to whisper dreams in her ear

She awakens from a drifting cloud
with a cherubim's kiss upon her face
Wandering innocently her ebony eyes
not looking past mother's embrace

Her laughter is the joy she feels
I adoring her beautiful smile
Her tears are her reason she gives
for growing, enlightening the child

She chases a rainbow, its colors
she's happy when she's left to roam
Only she can visit tomorrow, today
other's hearts is her home

She is content being alone
she wanders when she wants a friend
One has touched her curious nature
when she wanders there again

Her innocence is her treasure for now
and all that we choose to see
Her guardian angel is beside her
the one angel that's walked with me

A sister sign, she is beyond her time
her precious heart and soul He'll keep
Her guardian angel will make sure
when she rests her down to sleep.

For Aisha Rajeeyah, a beautiful child who is a
joy and GOD's gift to all who love her.

*C*over like a baby's blanket
*O*nly warmth my arms hold
*M*y love, a storybook untold
*P*urple passion lost in a dream
A fantasy with no way out
*S*o, I awaken with a child's pout
*S*ad to think his eyes are blinded
*I*nside another's wanting cries
*O*n he feels, out of my eyes
*N*ear Venus somewhere I find
A compatible nature, loneliness
*T*o match an empty heart as this
*E*ven now I'm still a child
*L*ike catching a butterfly, I'll try until
*Y*esterday I touched him, tomorrow I will…

Interlude from a Child's Heart

Winter's Flame

winter was cold, it has gone
you left me with a glowing flame
to warm my heart until fall

the seasons changed, so have I
fall has brought on many shades
has also colored me

though winter is fast approaching
no longer I need your warmth
I'll survive on winter's flame aglow

What is This Thing Called Love?

I wouldn't call it just
love
evolving and revolving
the sun, the moon and the stars
amiss in its abyss
of our own imagination
that surrenders to
a one syllable
emotion driven
heartache
not just love
two one's entwined
or should I say tangled
better yet, mangled
like heart strings
played until they're warped
or like the strings of a harp
when they begin
to play love's end
ah, there's that sacred word again
we open our hearts
bare our souls
aren't we vulnerable now
saying come what may
chances?
yes, I would love
and be loved again
so what is this thing called love?
should we ascertain it
or just rename it

but what if we claim it
and can't sustain it
stop me, please!
what am I doing in love?
am I?
I must have gotten lost
it's a place, too?
sure, why not
this love thing
careless to our rhythm and rhyme
how is it we can't escape it
or define the feeling?
just a feeling?
I wouldn't call it just a feeling…

In Touch

We're never alone
look inside
there's someone there
wanting to be reached
but not of a distance
are we afraid
to learn of ourselves
feeling ashamed when
we hear of ourselves
you think escape
to where and to what?
for the time being?
being what, wasted?
don't leave you behind
I hear someone yearning
don't trip this time
relate to reality
after all
it's down to earth
loneliness
that's in a trip
going to nowhere
coming back to emptiness
what a way to go
your inner being
know not of you
feeling worthless inside
what are you outside
but a reflection.

Free

I stroll along the edge of the shore
moving with the waters
kicking up particles embedded in the sand
alone once more
pieces of shattered seashells
digging into my every step
vying for my attention
not succeeding
waves racing to a finish
at my feet
keeping me company
the wind seems to say
come with me
let it free
I open my arms
it lifts me up over the sea
it whirls me within its grasp
never letting hold
but leaving me on my own
all at once I feel lightened
something has left me
that the wind now possesses
a friendly breeze settles me
all is calm
the waters are motionless
I find myself
picking up the scattered seashells
putting them in place
free once more.

Understanding...

Men...

It's part of their nature we don't understand
naturally, that's part of being a man
No brother likes to be evaluated
ladies, just accept what they demonstrated.

Women...

Well, why bother asking
who says we must be understood?
As long as intentions between are decent
the incomprehension may prove to be good.

There's More To Nature Than...

birds harmonizing
the sun and laughter of children synthesizing
the wind running, caught by the trees
the flow of water falling with ease
blades of grass reaching for the sky
feeling tears of clouds wondering why
holes in heavens floor at dusk
the sun not wanting to fade but must
for Mr. Moon will carry on
keeping his face visible till dawn
beasts of the earth eager to roam
never losing trail for everywhere is home
there's more to nature than sunshine and rain
there's human nature, the joy and pain.

These Eyes

These eyes become me, never deceiving
Only to those who risk unbelieving
Smiling eyes, laughter to be seen
A vague wandering coming from a dream
Haze of brown tinted by an olive shade
A hue of color distinctively made
These eyes seductive in a sexy fashion
Beneath them hides an eternity of passion
These eyes always searching for a place I can hold
Where I can see the truth, not hear or be told
It is often not easy to meet other's constant stare
Most times they're welcomed, some take a harmless glare
It is all important what I see, I know this is true
For if they're all you can see, these eyes are looking right through you.

Letter with Lines

I sit down to write you
a letter
more like
the bleeding of my heart
stained on paper
paper with lines
I depend on lines
they give strength
to these heavy sentiments
when I can't

It hurts, this opening
bleeding usually does
nothing like the pain
that comes from within
feeling without
could be the truth hurts
maybe this letter
with lines
hurts you, too?
yes, that is what I want

Raining
can't you feel it?
sterling teardrops
misty me
no, you can't
drip
drip
another stain

from inside out
maybe now?

I sit down to write you
this letter with lines
I can help you
read between them
but there's more unsaid
that can't be read
I can take the lines away
the sterling teardrops
but, then the bleeding stops
yes, that is what you want.

Someday I'll Fly Away

As free as the sea wind
to keep me within
the love I can't escape
I cannot confine
a love not mine
spare me the wait
Someday I'll fly away
leave your love to yesterday
make you a memory
One day I'll let go
wanting you to know
still, I'm not free
My aspirations wane
nothing stays the same
we must carry on
Without what could be
just think of me
when I'm gone
Someday I'll fly away
only to say
it's hurt I fear
One day I'll return
only to have learned
all in love is fair
Remember
the way we were
will always be
We shared a love

we weren't sure of
conditionally
Someday I'll make you a memory…
Someday I'll fly away.

In Search of. . .

Have you ever tried to look at something clearly
but fogginess distorts your vision,
haziness in any way, shape or form
masking what you so desperately need to see
knowing something is there but so obscure
you begin to doubt if it ever really was at all?

Ever try to brighten something you know has lost its shine
once was radiant, illuminating
but dimness now prevails
acknowledging what it was before and how its
mere presence left an enduring impression
that made you remember its shine?

Ever depend on something always being there
lasting you can touch, strong you can feel
suddenly disappearing, not a scent left behind
not a clue to find where it has gone or why
not even a shadow but a lingering on…
a faded stillness of what once was there?

Have you ever had a reality get foggy, dim, then disappear?

Ballroom

You danced your way into my heart
you took me by the hand and led me to the ballroom
in a moment I was in your arms learning your style
very close to you
Is that why they call you what they do?
I love the way you hold me
it feels oh, so good to hold you, too
making love would only be better, but if the music never ended
I could dance with you forever
How can I forget the first time or the song that was playing
What happens 'After the Love Has Lost its Shine'
or after we stop dancing?
Another time you held me close
and led me through the Ballroom
'Make it Last Forever', yes, sometimes I wish we could
but our last dance always lingers in my memory
until then…
until we Ballroom again.

The Runway

She dreamt of this world when she was a girl
a world of high fashion, high heels
and high expectations
a world visited through pages of a magazine
she lived her life
through that world of broken dreams...
Her face on the cover made to perfection
her body styling the latest collection
her image a distorted reflection
of the beauty other's eyes behold
She came as she was, with
Paris, France inspired hair
with waves like on the French Riviera
long as the Egypt's Nile
but worn Atlanta, Georgia style
A rendezvous swept her away
over the river and under the stars in her eyes
His name was French, or she wanted it to be
not part of her dream, though she was intrigued
he was part of that world she couldn't conceive
New York, New York
she made her way to that world he lives
not on the cover of her dreams
but in the bed of his
She awakens
eyes are set, lips are pursed
attitude in check as if she cursed
fashion uncompromised
lights and music synchronized
destination...

The Runway
Legs prancing like a deer in stride
hands perched on her hips
swaying from side to side
stepping to the beat of her own heart
She stops…poses…steps…turns
confidently exhibiting what she learned
commentator reading her like a fashion magazine
punctuating her every move
not turning the page till the crowd approves
And did she say this sister was "Fierce?!"
She spreads her arms wide as an eagle's wings
hovering over the crowd as if they were prey
pivoting like a mannequin frozen in motion
under the allure of some magic potion
She stops…poses…steps…turns
eruption from the crowd as she comes alive again
and this world of broken dreams ends on
The Runway.

A Matter of the Heart

It started with a look amidst familiar faces
a look that gave voice to unspoken words
we couldn't say, we shouldn't feel
feeling you without touching me
drawn to each other like a magnet
an attraction not permeating our touch
but manipulating our minds
to surrender our bodies to each other
we were powerless to stop it
or were we?
And what did the heart matter?
for this wasn't a matter of the heart
but a passion of the flesh
and a betrayal of who we were
amidst familiar faces
there was one who thought she knew
our familiar faces, too
I knew you beyond yourself
I knew the better half of you
whose heart did matter in this
We met in secret places
found hidden hours, kept stolen moments
we changed your name to make you
more mysterious than we were to each other
and not the same man she knew
he was married and you were too
and I was invincible beyond us both

you ended every goodbye with this
"Take care of your sweet and lovely self"
but our first hello was the beginning of the end
for us.

A Woman Defined

How can I tell you
the ways of a woman
being a woman
not understanding myself
I give you myself as I am
if any other would dare
let them compare
You stand tall
within yourself you know you must
saying, "I am a man!"
I agree; you stand tall
you love me
I AM A WOMAN!!
Not to be wavering in my stance
whether political, ethical or nonsense
but to be unapologetic
prophetic
poetic
and understood
Not to be defined by any definition
or explanation of my own volition
but to be the sum of me
you do the addition
Being me
is my only ambition
and all there is to understanding
In my desire to be
Ms. Understood

I have felt you watching me
thinking… 'She is a woman!'
I AGREE; I AM A WOMAN!!
JUST LOVE ME!!

When Will I Ever Be Enough...

Not for me
I think I'm quite complete
and very much a lady with a capital
L-A-D-Y
and in every way the word can be defined
yes, for me I'm quite enough
and just a little bit more
No, not for me
the selected few who were once a part of me
and those who have yet to leave a part of themselves
gentlemen (in every way the word can be defined)
whom I've adored, respected, sometimes loved
whom were intelligent, sexy, sometimes insecure
sometimes about me
they were sure I wasn't enough for them
I was sure I was
maybe I was too much for them
just doing what a lady does
These gentlemen (sometimes insecure)
I could have made complete
(if only they didn't feel the need to look elsewhere).

For Coco

We've known each other
since we were pimple-faced teenagers
when nothing else mattered, not even boys
we girls had each other, back then it was enough
when everything was fun and laughter
there weren't many tears
only when our mothers intervened
remember how we hated that?
growing up was hard to do without trying

****

One summer there was an interlude between us
that melted into summers after that
during that time I was wondering
where do I go from here, how do I get there
you, I guess wondering the same thing
but in a different place
this was the one time we were without each other

****

Years later and everything mattered
we came of age
smoother complexions and boys were our toys
even better, they grew up too!
to me it was more of an awakening
this coming of age
reality can be startling coming out of being a kid
you seem to have taken it as well as I

it was fun being a kid but I'm glad
I'm not a kid anymore…what about you?

****

We renewed our friendship which never ended
we came together and shared notes
we've taken so far in this course
lessons learned, mistakes made, aspirations
we discovered pain and loss
there were more tears than before
we shared those, too

****

Fun and laughter became "Disco Nights!"
I never knew how much fun you were to party with
and those sexy party dresses
sometimes, girlfriend, you amazed me!
I loved the way you hollered, "Party over here!!"
it always made me laugh and I would say to myself,
'Yes indeed, those Black Russians
have taken her hostage!'
you are definitely a "Disco Queen" in my book

****

Our sisters who we grew up with have gone away
I guess to find their places, too
leaving us with memories to cherish for a lifetime
missing them, but wishing them well
both of us wondering will we ever see them again
and hoping they too, remember

****

Today, you and I we're still together
after all these years we've weathered through the worst
and came out with the best friendship
two women can share
we've been through so much together
shared almost everything
we've been there for each other when the guys
didn't act right, when the sun didn't always shine
the rain got heavy at times
but you and I were there

****

This is for you, Coco
for remaining your true color
when things got a little shady
and for making our friendship and absolute joy to me
I couldn't have done it alone
You are a beautiful black woman,
my sister, and the best friend
a girl could have traveled with through the years.

Don't Cry for Me
(A SONG)

Yesterday
you made my heart melt
the feelings you always said you'd felt
I've given you so much of me
my love, for all eternity
you gave me a destiny
a forever time and place to be
Today
I've lost everything I've gained
my lifeline for which my love sustained
you said there was someone else who
needed you more, how could this be true
you tearfully try to ease my pain
but the tears you cry are tears in vain

****

Baby, don't cry for me
all I can see are the tears
but is the pain for real
Baby, let my heartache be
it's in my mind a memory
of a love and sadness I'll always feel

****

If this is what you want to be
I'm asking you please don't cry for me

****

What couldn't I do for you
that you needed another to pull you through
I'll never understand why or give freely again
my love to another man when
I love you, and its where I want to belong
taking your love away is so very wrong

****

Baby, please don't cry for me
although I'm weak from misery
I know my strength is above me
Baby, listen, don't shed a tear
all I really want to hear
is that you'll stay and love me

****

A rainy day can never equally
match the tears you cry for me
but is the pain you feel for real
No, no don't cry for me
I need your love, not tears or pity
no apologies or sorrow
I need your touch lasting tomorrow
I love you baby, can't you see
but I don't want you to cry for me…

I Wonder

I have loved and I have lost
it was easy to let go; it hurt but not too much
no tears or heartache
So, I wonder...
did I ever really love these men
and was I every really loved again?

I found a truer love when I found myself
this love only I could give me
and it could never be taken away
So, I wonder...
did I ever really need another
to give me the love that I discovered?

I have let another love me
and I can't seem to let go, though I have tried
Have I loved again?
So, I wonder...
is this where I finally belong
the place I've wondered about for so long?

Mom

You were forever my strength
Sometimes my own two feet
I have stumbled many times
But you never let me fall
There were times you never knew
I have been brought to my knees
I picked myself up, dusted me off
Without letting you see my pain
Without letting my bruises show
Not wanting to burden you more
But still needing you so

Mom,
I ask myself if you were ever happy
And if I really wanted know
I saw your pain; your bruises showed
You, too, were brought to your knees
I remember the battles you fought
Seems we both battled alone
Or so it seems we thought
But your spirit was never broken
And you battled to the end
Those outside forces, the dark places within
And we who were righteous and just
Still, you were victorious
For the joy of the Lord became your strength
And happy became glad
For the peace you never had
And for forgiveness
I know you prayed for my soul

With this world I was obsessed
I pray I've brought you joy in Heaven
For, now I am saved and blessed

Mom,
I hope your heart was guarded
Against the selfish young girl
Neither of us could escape
And I hope somewhere
In those dark places within her
You saw light
You felt love.

Remembrance

Where do I begin to remember
or do I forget
and ignore the emptiness in my heart
that I cannot fill
with more memories that I have of you
because they came to an end
When I begin to remember
do I laugh or smile
or do I just cry and let the warmth
of those memories comfort me
I never want to forget
or forget to remember
your laugh, your smile
they are mine now
When I look down at my hands
I see yours
when I look at me
I see you
when I think of you
I remember
and if I don't let them end
the memories I have of you
will fill my empty heart again
I never thought I'd ever be without you.

Keeping House in Heaven

Mother,
you left us a long time ago
your spirit remained with us
but we never left you though
we could still see you
through eyes that are yours
still hold your hand
that lay bare many chores
still touch your face
untouched by the years erased
years we faced without you
still caress your hair
that was as dark and long
as the night without the face of the moon
but, still we miss you

So, I return in my mind
where I know I would find you
to a humble start where I left my heart
to a place called "Mother's"
because you were always there
I remember
your salt and pepper seasoned hair
peeking out
under a loosely tied kerchief
over smooth Irish skin and some Indian
I kiss your face and smell your scent again

I remember
your hand sewn aprons

hugged every dress you wore
tied around hips I used to ask for (and got!)
I return to the aroma of coffee
early morning that woke up the day
to chicken and dumplings
turnip greens picked fresh
homemade chicken soup prepared and blessed
fried cornbread cooked in lard
peaches marinating in mason jars
and home-made-with-love applesauce
(if nostalgia had an aroma it would smell like your kitchen)

I return to freshly washed sheets
held high on long wooden pegs
billowing in the wind and running from our little legs
in the "rec-room"
(which could have been named in our honor)
I find you starching, ironing, folding clothes
as you Search for Tomorrow with your Guiding Light
and what you're doing now, I suppose
sometimes I would find you
in the garden behind the shed
your straw hat tied underneath your chin
your sneakers comfortably worn-in
preparing the vegetables' bed

And still yet I see you
studying at the dining table
you went back to school, how cool!
even though you were not able
Sunday, you said, was the "Lord's Day"
that same chair you studied in
Sunday became your pew
your Bible open to hear His Word

spoken out of view
you never left your sanctuary
He just brought Heaven and earth to you

So, I return again and again
to that big white country home
you served many that came through that door
now your serving only One
you're keeping house in Heaven.

'I thank my God upon every remembrance of you'
Philippians 1:3

Yesterday

I would have been with you
Yesterday
If tomorrow had come sooner
I only know the days between
Wouldn't have made time for us
If we'd found each other then

I would have been with you
Today
I might not have waited for
Tomorrow
For it may have never come
If only I had known you then
I would have been with you.

My Knight in Armor

I watch you, follow you
with my eyes
your stature so commanding
yet gentle and strong
your presence frames my body
stills my world
leaves me captured
your eyes permeate my soul
your voice resonates inside me
Barry White style
deep down
and I feel you

Your mellow
like the brandy you sip
dark, smooth, intoxicating
Yeah
or cognac, sexy and warm
like your body, warm and sexy
my lips drip
sweet honey-suckle juices
when your lips taste me
intoxicating…
Yeah
just like the brandy you sip

You are a ladies' gentleman
the perfect man
for an imperfect woman
like me

how special am I
that you chose to love me
how gallant are you
my knight in shining armor
you have battled for me
sacrificing yourself
never surrendering

I honor you with this
my knight in armor
I honor you with my life
that you battled me for
and won
love has conquered
and I succumb
my gentle warrior
keep me imprisoned in your heart
captive where you love
and I will never escape.

Bridges over Time

I have lived
in the presence of others
and in the passage from
one bridge to another
suspended over time
Expressions of a Life
flowed like a river
and over the depths of a canyon
these bridges over time remain

I have loved (not been loved)
in my whimsical world
with not a sober mind
but inquisitive spirit
a life stolen
from the prying feline
I've danced the Ballroom
crossed the galaxy on a star
and discovered the universe

On the runway
I lived my dream
reality was not what it seemed
and winter was cold
I declared, "I AM A WOMAN!"
"OK, A BITCH!"
"LOVE ME ANYWAY!"
and I wandered my way
into forbidden domain
at what cost does one
render themselves invincible?

I revisit those bridges
not passing over
not compromising the years
leaving them as I found them
like pieces of scattered seashells
buried in sand
The treasures of the universe
nurture the treasures of my soul
they are priceless
and they too, remain with time

In time
I affirmed, "I am a L-A-D-Y"
mailed that letter with lines
went in search of
discovered that I was enough
and finally found
what that thing called love is.

Lightning Source UK Ltd.
Milton Keynes UK
UKHW012057020123
414736UK00011B/168/J